RECORDED VERSIONS
GUITAR ®
AUTHENTIC TRANSCRIPTIONS
WITH NOTES AND TABLATURE

THE BEST OF
Cheap Trick

Rick Nielsen, guitars

Robin Zander, vocals

Tom Petersson, 12-string bass

Bun E. Carlos, drums

Back cover photo by Mark Seliger
Photos courtesy of the Cheap Trick archives.

This publication is not for sale in
the E.C. and/or Australia
or New Zealand.

ISBN 0-7935-4458-0

HAL•LEONARD®
CORPORATION
7777 W. BLUEMOUND RD. P.O. BOX 13819 MILWAUKEE, WI 53213

THE BEST OF Cheap Trick

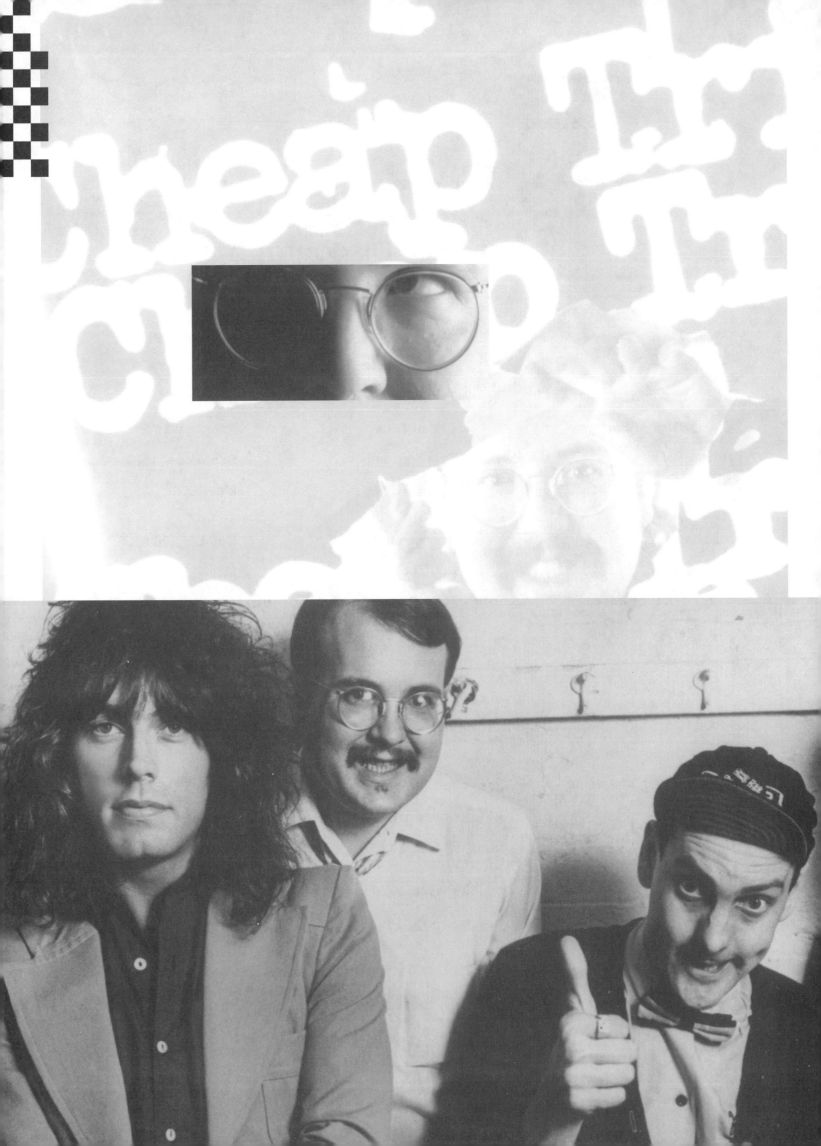

Cheap Trick
U.S.A. Discography

Title	Producer	Released
Cheap Trick	Jack Douglas	February 1977
In Color	Tom Werman	August 1977
Heaven Tonight	Tom Werman	May 1978
Cheap Trick at Budokan	Cheap Trick	February 1979
Dream Police	Tom Werman	September 1979
Found All The Parts (10-inch "Nu-Disk")	Cheap Trick	May 1980
All Shook Up	George Martin	October 1980
One On One	Roy Thomas Baker	May 1982
Next Position Please	Todd Rundgren	August 1983
Standing On The Edge	Jack Douglas	June 1985
The Doctor	Tony Platt	September 1986
Lap Of Luxury	Richie Zito	April 1988
Busted	Richie Zito	July 1990
Cheap Trick's Greatest Hits	Various	September 1991
Woke Up With A Monster	Ted Templeman	March 1994
Budokan II	Cheap Trick	July 1994
Christmas CD	Cheap Trick	December 1995

And many soundtracks, too numerous to mention.

Compilation Video: *Every Trick In The Book* — July 1990

Ain't That a Shame (Live)

Words and Music by Antoine Domino and Dave Bartholomew

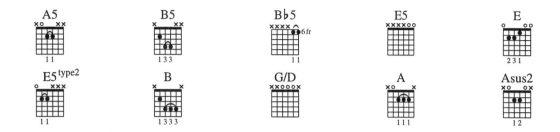

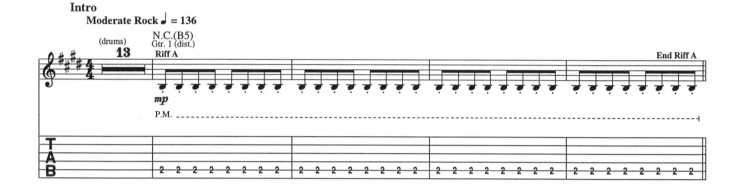

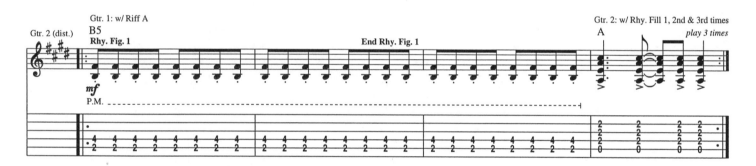

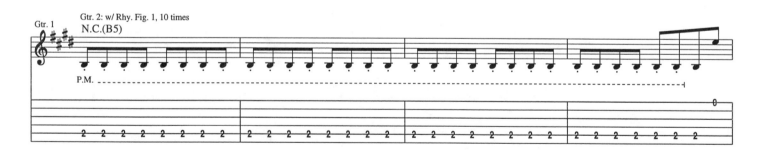

Coda 1
Guitar Solo

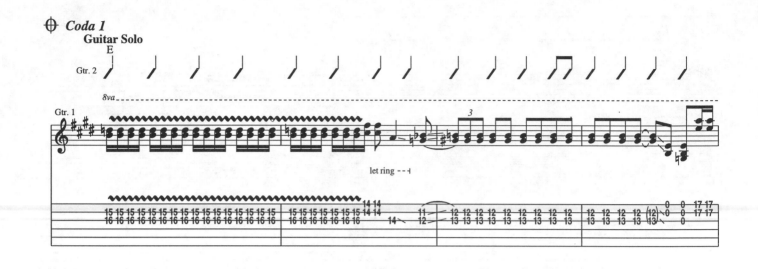

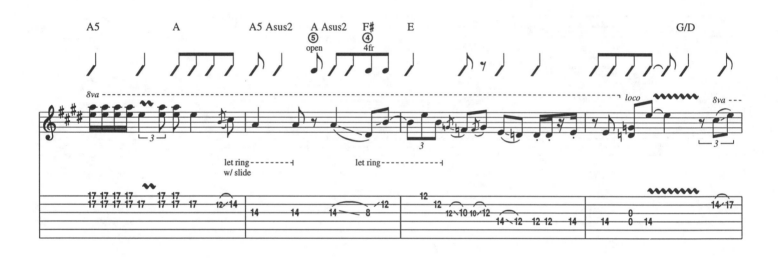

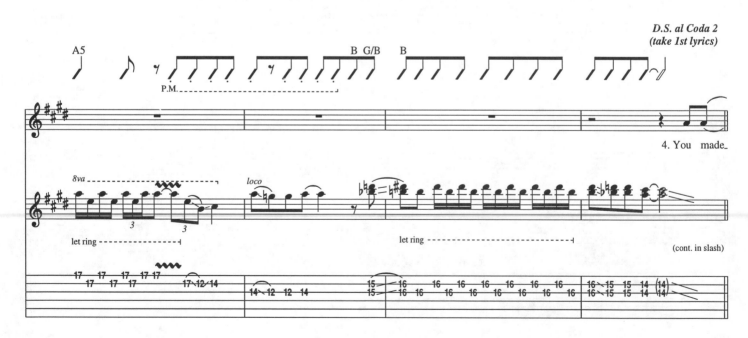

Outro

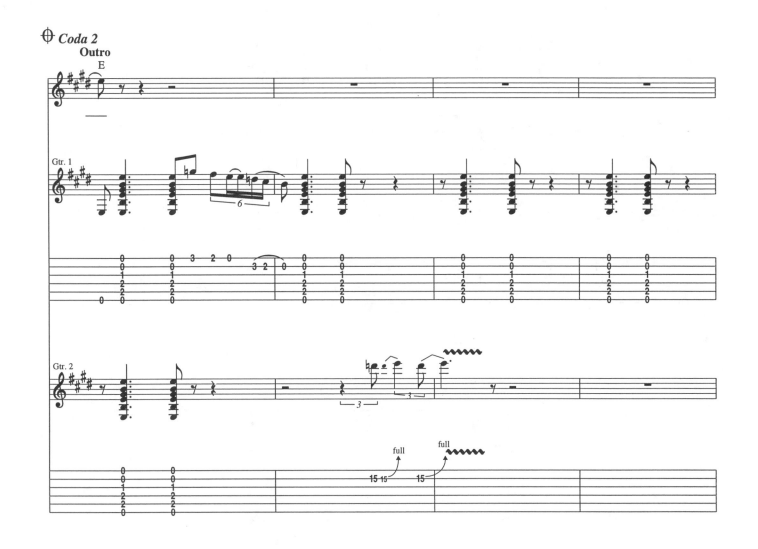

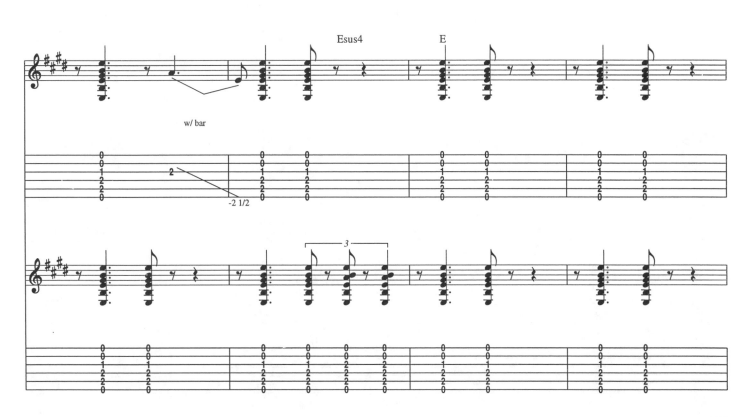

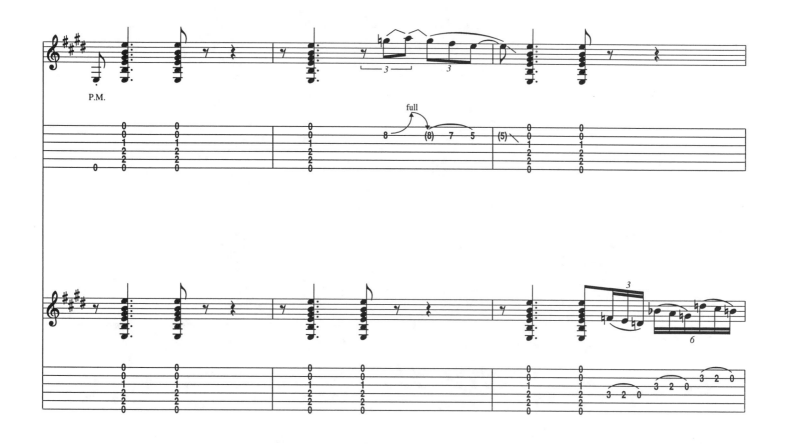

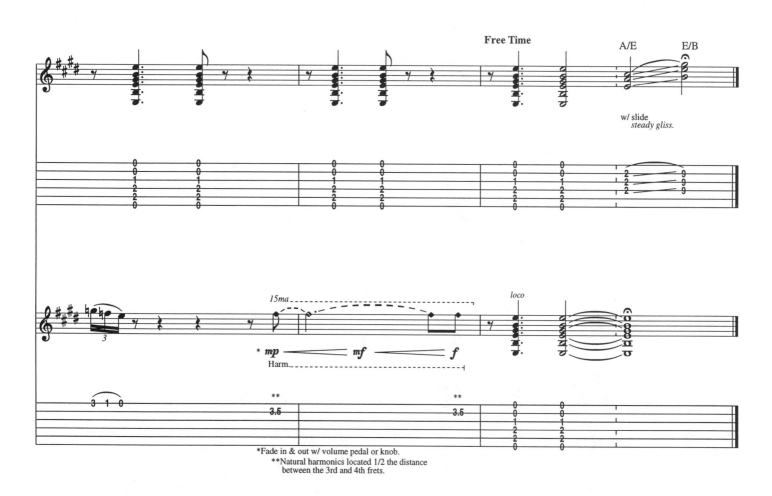

*Fade in & out w/ volume pedal or knob.
  **Natural harmonics located 1/2 the distance
    between the 3rd and 4th frets.

California Man

Written by Roy Wood

Well, my legs start to shiv-er when I

hear you call my name.— I'm a Cal-i-for-ni-a man,— yeah.—

Guitar Solo

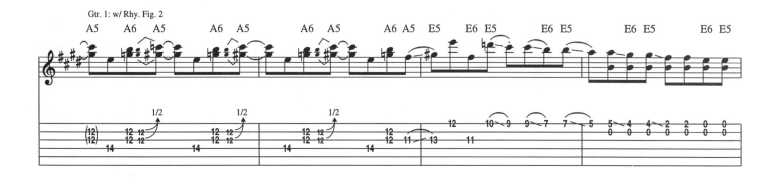

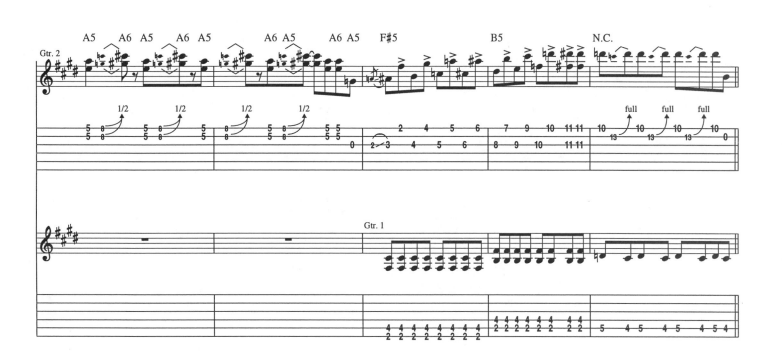

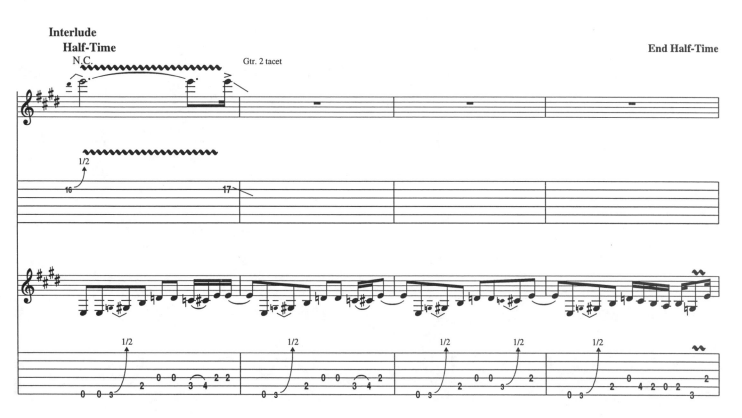

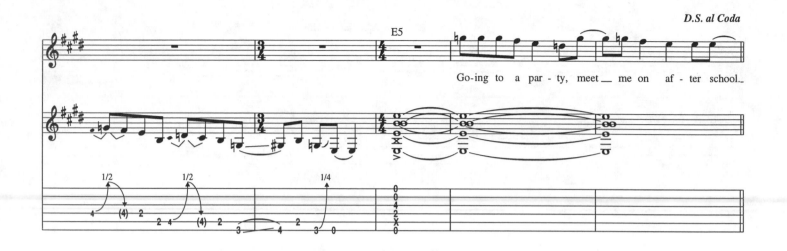

D.S. al Coda

Go-ing to a par - ty, meet __ me on af - ter school. __

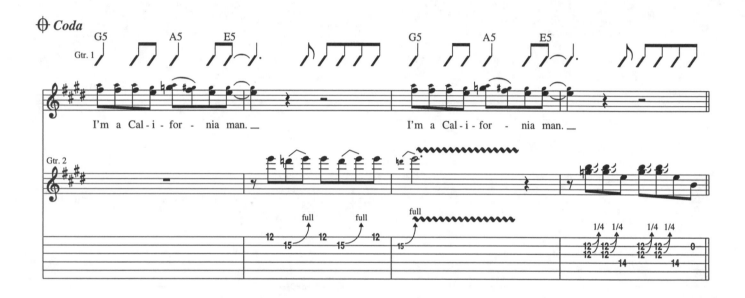

⊕ **Coda**

I'm a Cal - i - for - nia man. __   I'm a Cal - i - for - nia man. __

Outro

let ring ------

Clock Strikes Ten

Words and Music by Rick Nielsen

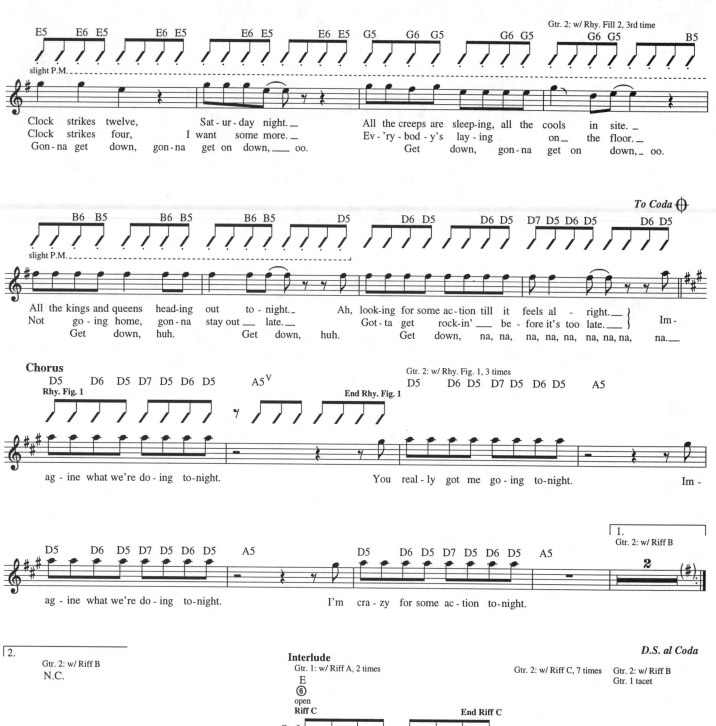

Clock strikes twelve, Sat - ur - day night.__ All the creeps are sleep-ing, all the cools in site.__
Clock strikes four, I want some more.__ Ev - 'ry - bod - y's lay - ing on__ the floor.__
Gon - na get down, gon - na get on down,__ oo.__ Get down, gon - na get on down,__ oo.

All the kings and queens head-ing out to - night.__ Ah, look-ing for some ac - tion till it feels al - right.__ }
Not go - ing home, gon - na stay out __ late.__ Got - ta get rock-in' __ be - fore it's too late.__ } Im - na
Get down, huh. Get down, huh. Get down, na, na, na, na, na, na, na, na, na.__

Chorus

ag - ine what we're do - ing to - night. You real - ly got me go - ing to - night. Im -

ag - ine what we're do - ing to - night. I'm cra - zy for some ac - tion to - night.

Ow. ____

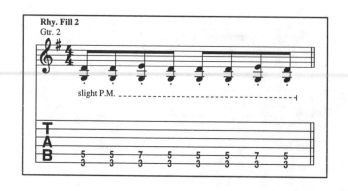

Day Tripper (Live)

Words and Music by John Lennon and Paul McCartney

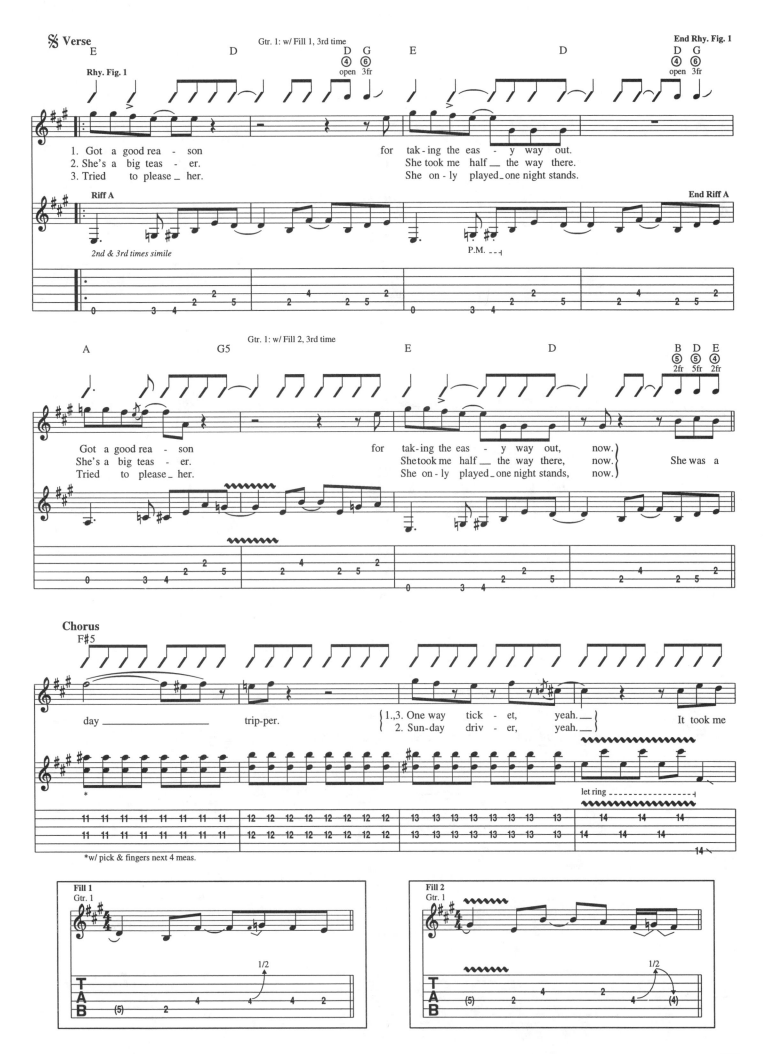

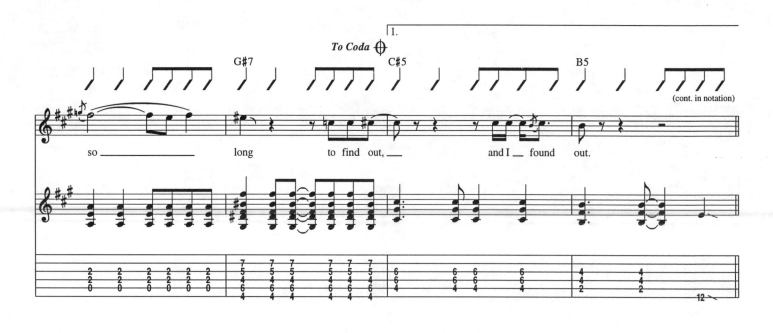

so _____ long   to find out, __   and I __ found   out.

Interlude

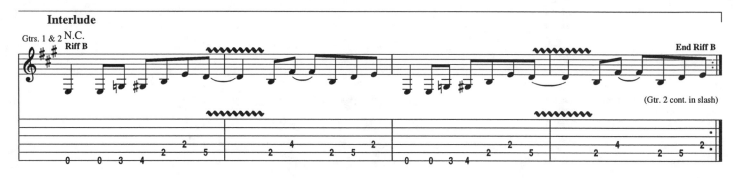

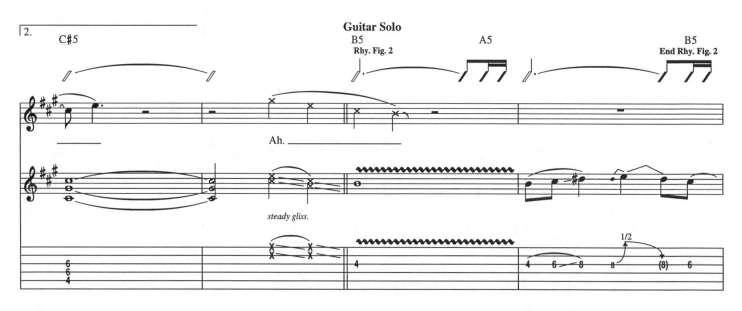

Guitar Solo

Gtr. 2: w/ Rhy. Fig. 2, 4 times, simile

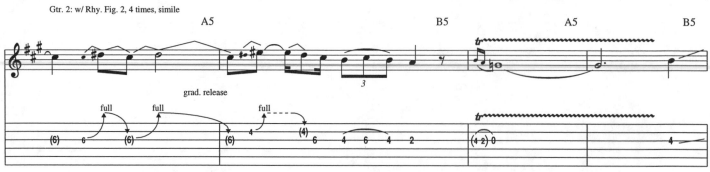

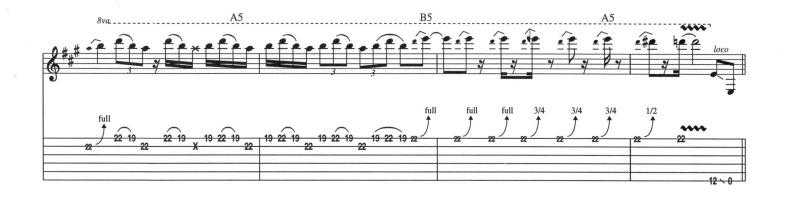

Interlude

Gtrs. 1 & 2: w/ Riff B

D.S. al Coda

Coda

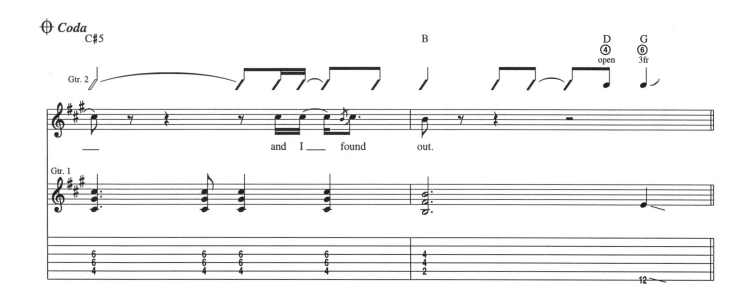

and I found out.

Interlude

Yeah, yeah, yeah.

And does.

Outro

Gtr. 1: w/ Rhy. Fill 1, 1st & 2nd times, simile
Gtr. 2: w/ Rhy. Fig. 1, simile
Gtr. 1: w/ Riff A, 3rd & 4th times, simile

Gtrs. 1 & 2: w/ Rhy. Fill 2, 1st time
Gtr. 1: w/ Riff A, 1st 2 meas, 2nd time, simile

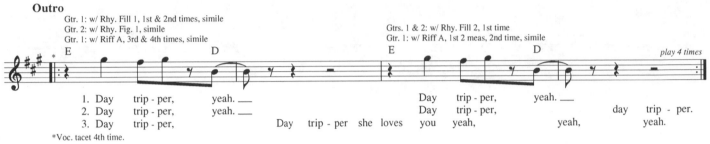

play 4 times

1. Day trip - per,   yeah. ___
2. Day trip - per,   yeah. ___
3. Day trip - per,

Day trip - per,   yeah. ___
Day trip - per,   day trip - per.
Day trip - per she loves you yeah,   yeah,   yeah.

*Voc. tacet 4th time.

Free Time

Dream Police

Words and Music by Rick Nielsen

*Chord symbols reflect implied tonality.

The Flame

Words and Music by Bob Mitchell and Nick Graham

Gtrs. 1 & 2: w/ Rhy. Figs. 2A

What - ev - er you want, ___ I'll give it to you. ___

When-ev-er you need _ some - one to lay your heart _ and head _ up-on, re-mem-ber: af - ter the fire, af - ter

Rhy. Fig. 3

Gtr. 1

Gtr. 2

P.M.

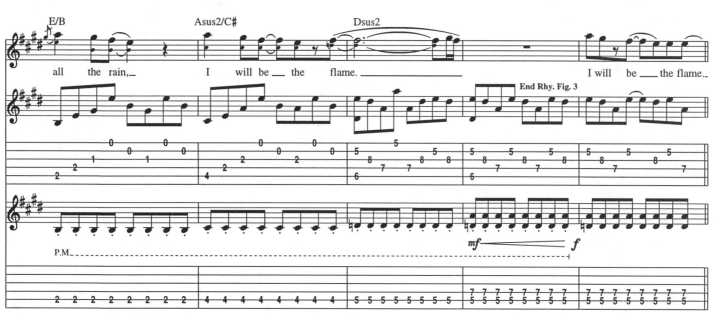

all the rain, _ I will be _ the flame. ___ I will be _ the flame. _

End Rhy. Fig. 3

P.M.

mf *f*

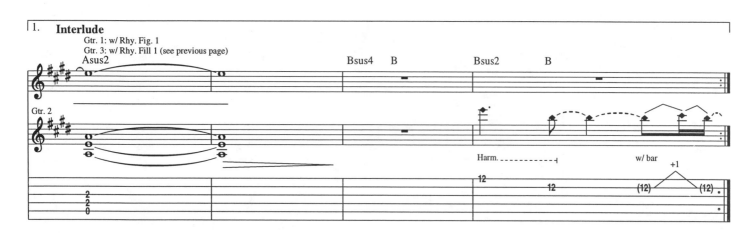

1. **Interlude**

Gtr. 1: w/ Rhy. Fig. 1
Gtr. 3: w/ Rhy. Fill 1 (see previous page)

Asus2   Bsus4   B   Bsus2   B

Gtr. 2

Harm.

w/ bar

+1

Girlfriends

Words and Music by Rick Nielsen, Robin Zander, Tom Petersson and Bun E. Carlos

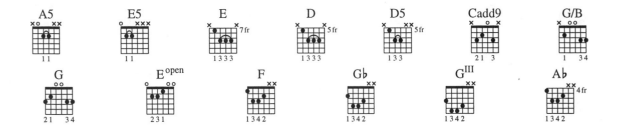

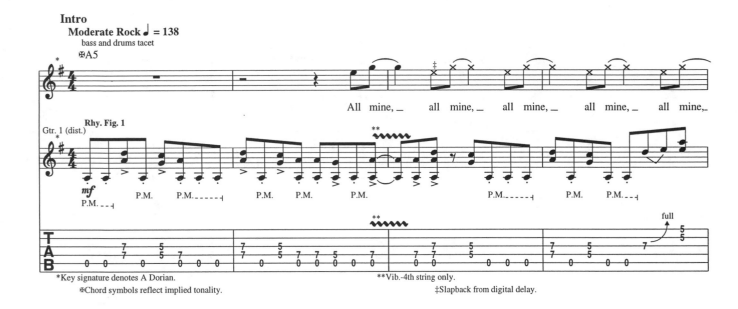

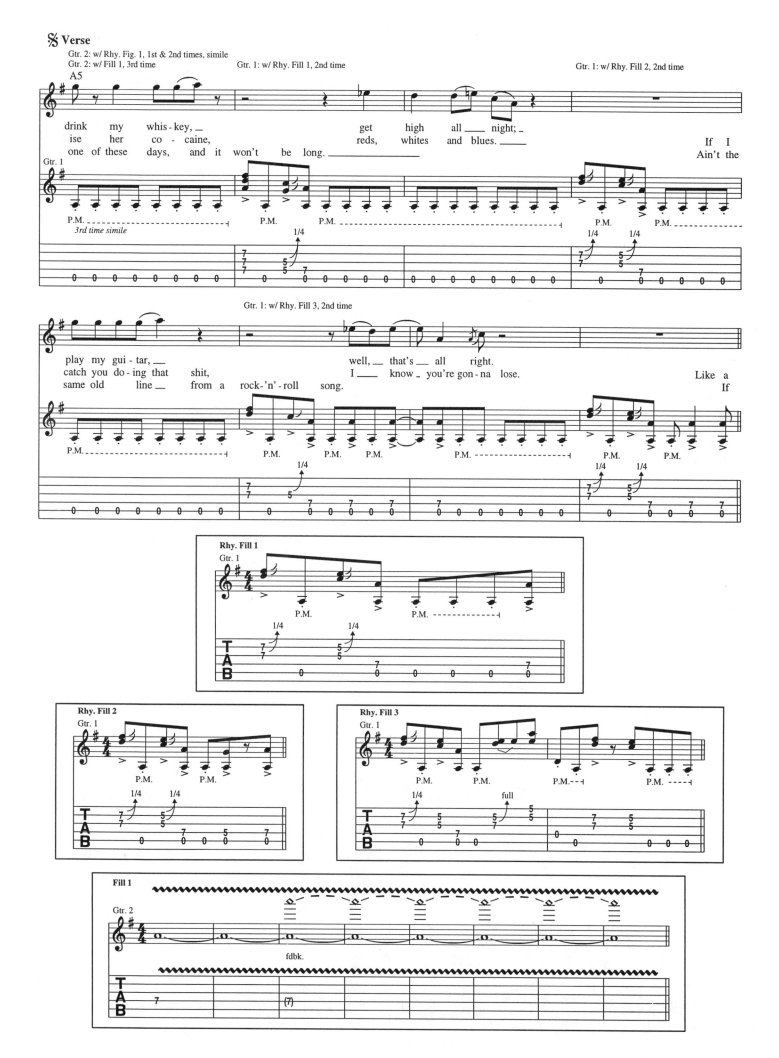

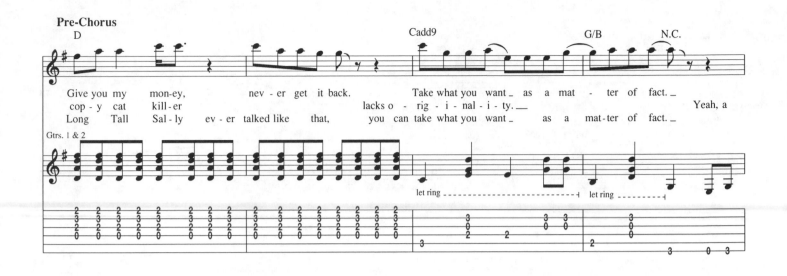

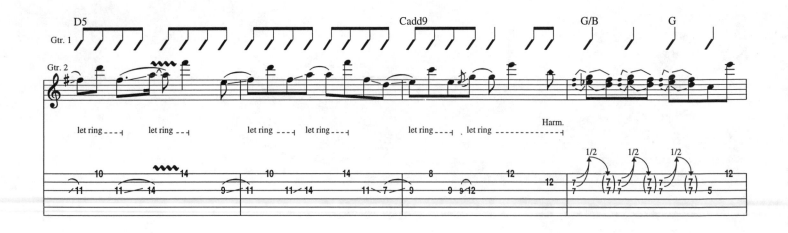

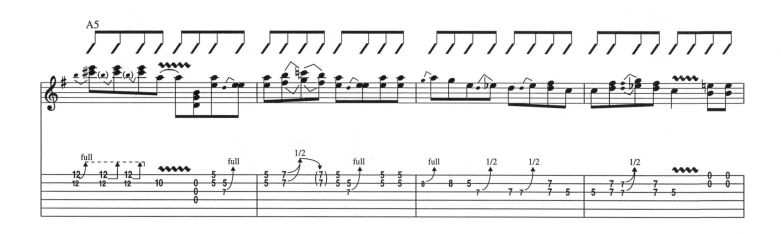

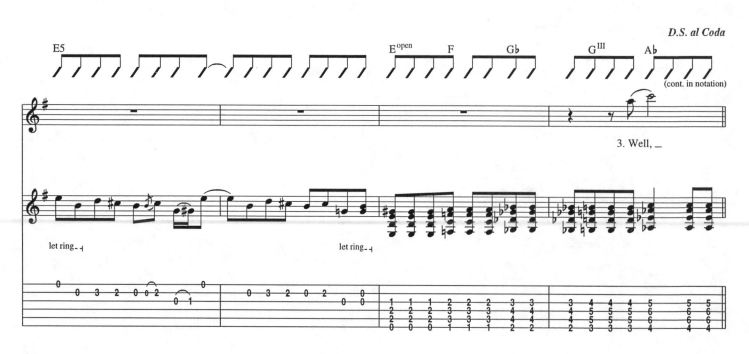

$\oplus$ *Coda*

Chorus

Gtr. 1: w/Rhy. Fig. 3A
Gtr. 2: w/Rhy. Fig. 3, 1st 6 meas.

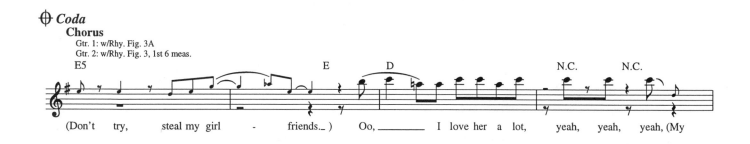

(Don't try, steal my girl - friends._) Oo, _____ I love her a lot, yeah, yeah, yeah, (My

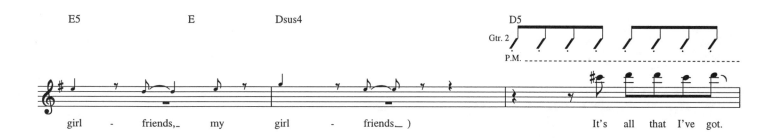

girl - friends,_ my girl - friends._) It's all that I've got.

It's all that I've got. _____ It's all that I've got, _____ oh, _____ yeah. _____

Gtr. 2: w/ Rhy. Fig. 2

Oh, yeah. _____ My

Outro

w/ voc. ad Libs. on repeats
Gtr. 2: w/ Rhy. Fig. 2, simile

Play 4 Times and Fade

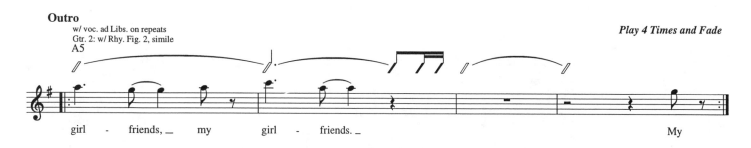

girl - friends, _ my girl - friends. _ My

Gonna Raise Hell

Words and Music by Rick Nielsen

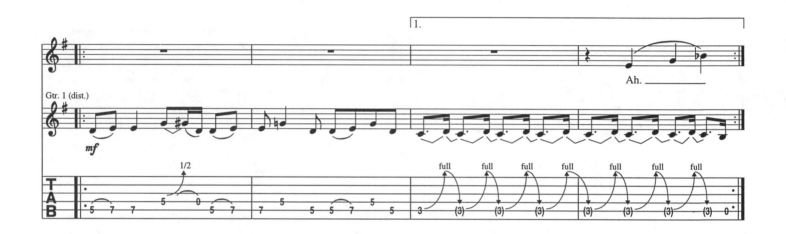

heard is true, there's noth-ing much I can do to change the world._ It's ir - re-vers - i - ble. _____ But in
won't name names, and a se-cret's a se - cret. But a hints a hint or a clue. _____ I real -
bod - y here, ev - 'ry - bod - y ___ here gets a fate, I, I'll a - gree, ___ oh. ___

*T = Thumb on ⑥

Rhy. Fill 2
Gtr. 1

Rhy. Fill 5
Gtr. 1

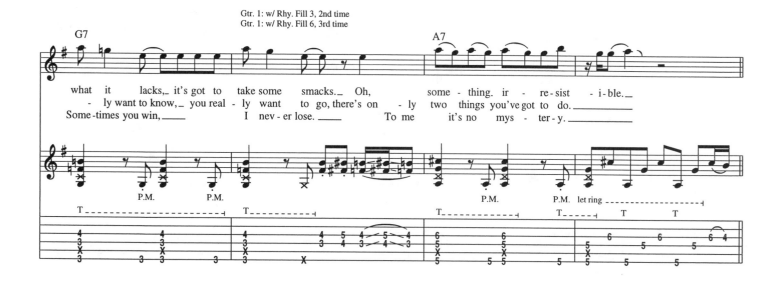

what it lacks,_ it's got to take some smacks._ Oh,   some - thing. ir - re - sist - i - ble._
\- ly want to know,_ you real - ly want to go, there's on - ly two things you've got to do.___
Some -times you win, ____ I nev - er lose. ____ To me it's no mys - ter - y. _____

Chorus

N.C.

Gon - na raise hell, gon - na raise hell, gon - na raise hell. _____

Riff B

End Riff B

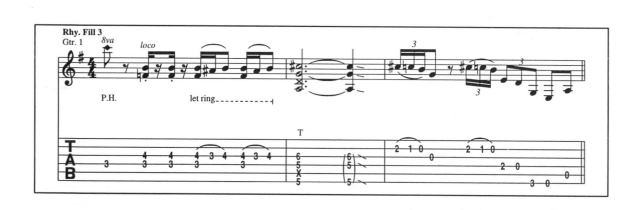

Rhy. Fill 3

Gtr. 1

Rhy. Fill 6

Gtr. 1

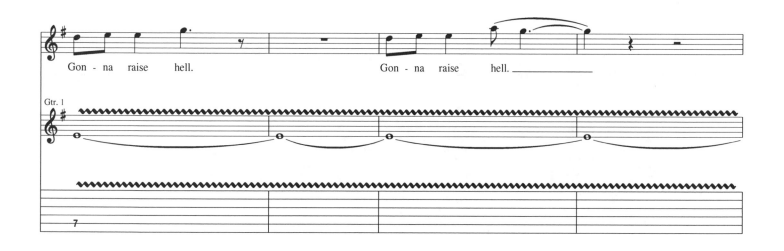

Gon - na raise hell. Gon - na raise hell.

Gtr. 1

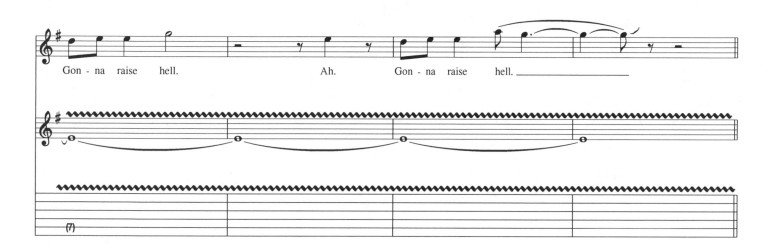

Gon - na raise hell. Ah. Gon - na raise hell.

Interlude

Gtr. 1: ad Lib, next 16 meas.
(drums & bass)

24

Guitar Solo

N.C.

Gtr. 1

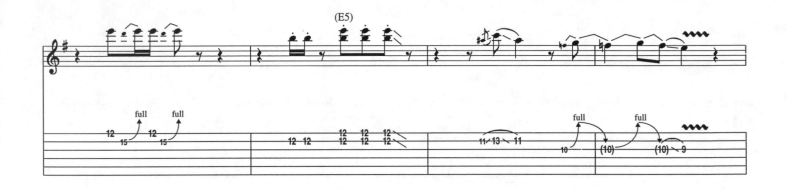

Outro

Play 7 Times and Fade

Hot Love

Words and Music by Rick Nielsen

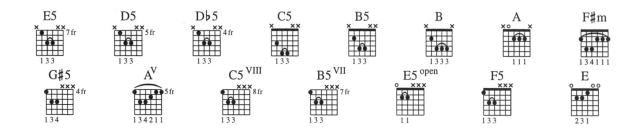

*Key signature denotes A Mixolydian.

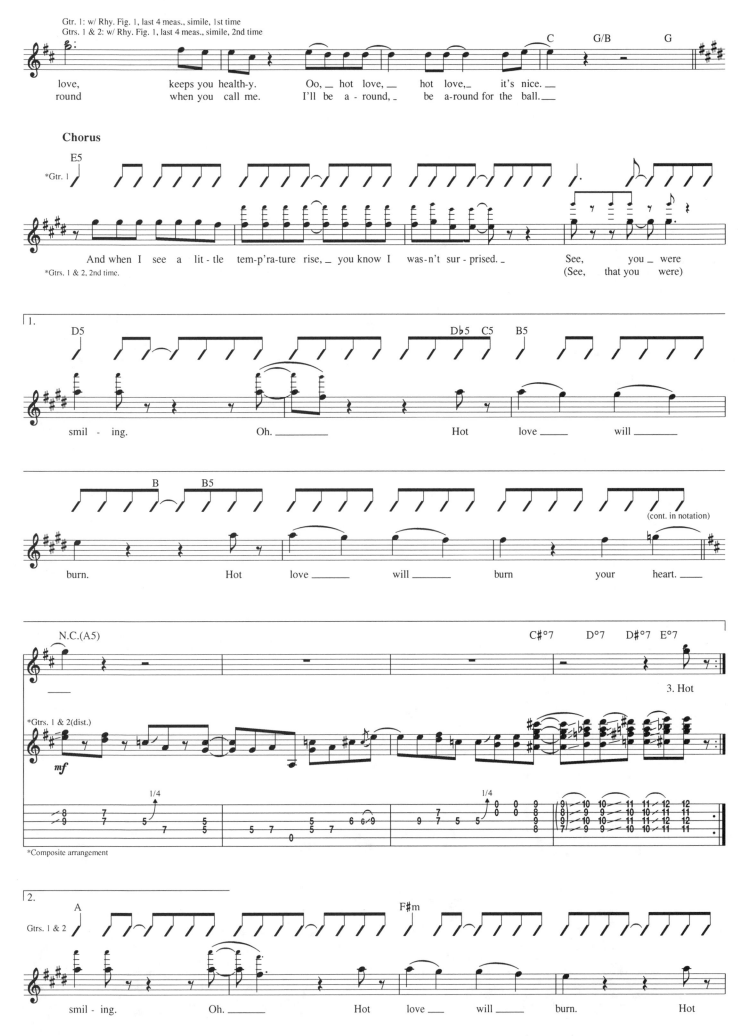

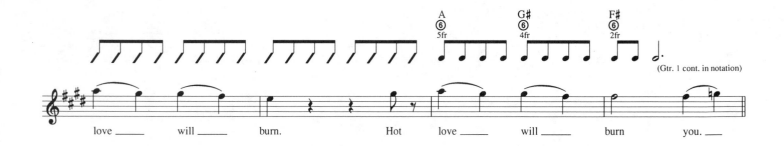

love ____ will ____ burn. Hot love ____ will ____ burn you. ____

(Gtr. 1 cont. in notation)

Bridge
Gtr. 2 tacet
N.C.

I'm sell - ing this, hot love for you, ____ and for you., I give it a - way.

Gtr. 1

P.M.

15ma. loco

*Harm.

*Natural harmonic is located 2/10 the distance between the 6th and 7th frets.

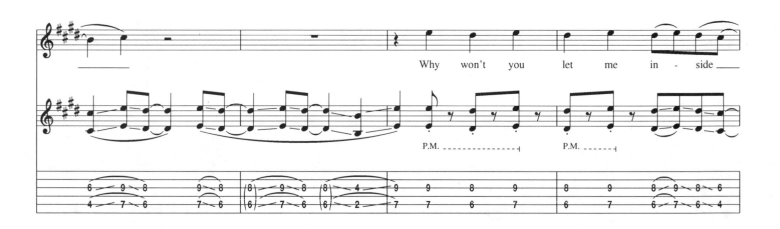

Why won't you let me in - side ____

P.M.   P.M.

____ of you ____ oh, to - nite? ____

15ma. loco

Harm. P.M.

full   full full full

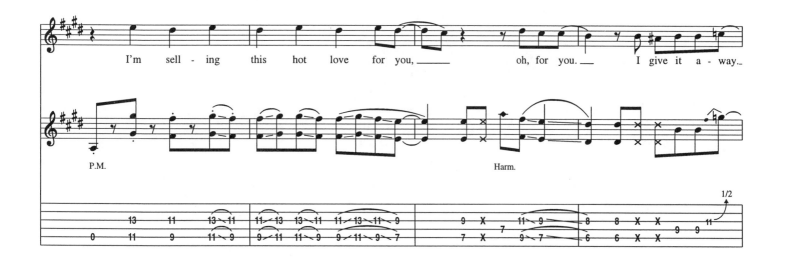

Outro-Chorus

love ____ will ____ burn.   Hot   love ____ will ____ burn   your   heart.

Hot

(cont. in slash)

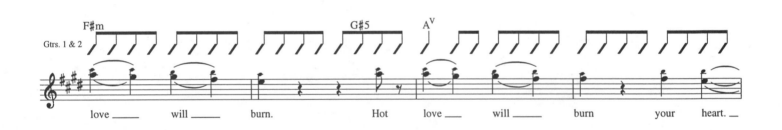

love ____ will ____ burn.   Hot   love ___ will ____ burn   your   heart. ___

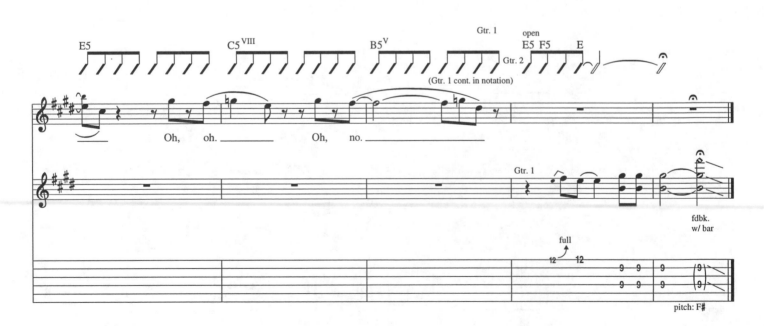

Oh,   oh. _____   Oh,   no. _____

I Want You To Want Me (Live)

Words and Music by Rick Nielsen

Pre-Chorus

Gtr. 1: w/ Rhy. Fig. 1, 1st 3 meas., simile
Gtr. 2: w/ Rhy. Fig. 1A, 2 times, simile

Guitar Solo

Gtr. 2: w/ Rhy. Fig. 1A, simile

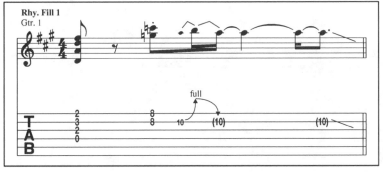

Rhy. Fill 1
Gtr. 1

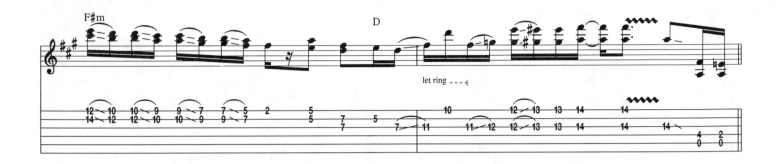

Pre-Chorus
Gtr. 2 tacet

Feel-in' all a-lone with-out a friend, you know you feel like dy - in'. _____ Oh, _____

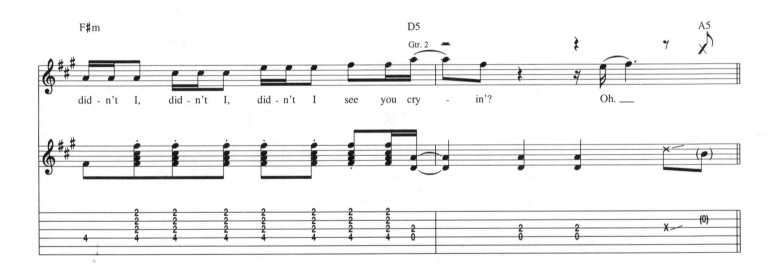

did - n't I, did - n't I, did - n't I see you cry - in'? Oh. ___

Guitar Solo
Gtr. 2: w/ Rhy. Fig. 1A, simile

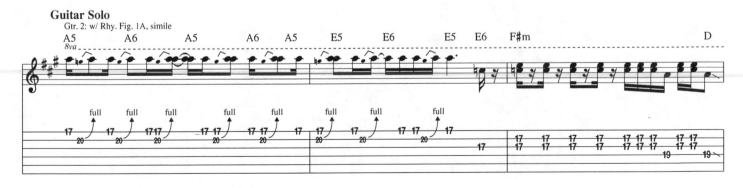

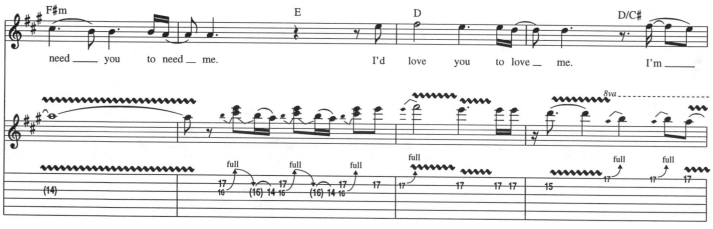

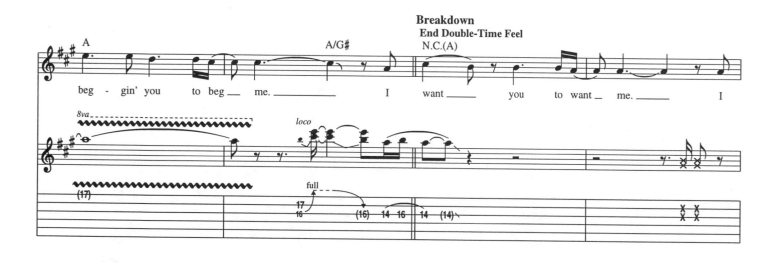

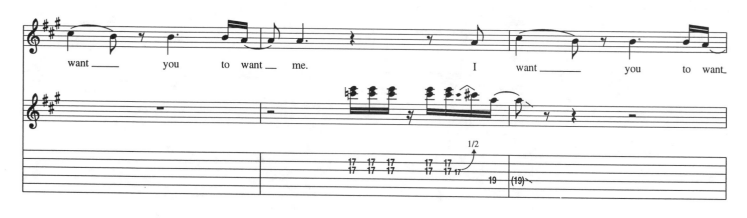

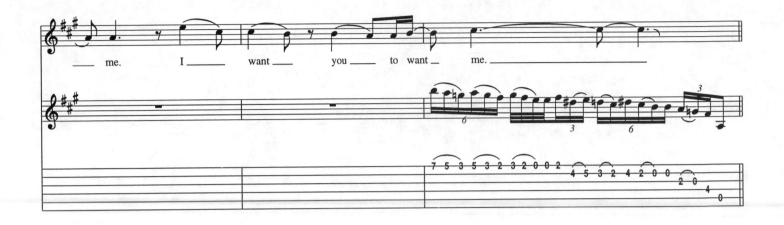

me. I ____ want ____ you ____ to want ____ me. ____

Outro
Double-Time Feel
N.C.(A)

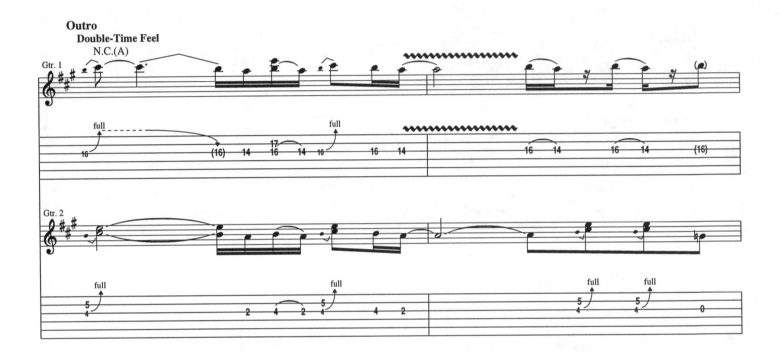

Free Time
End Double-Time Feel

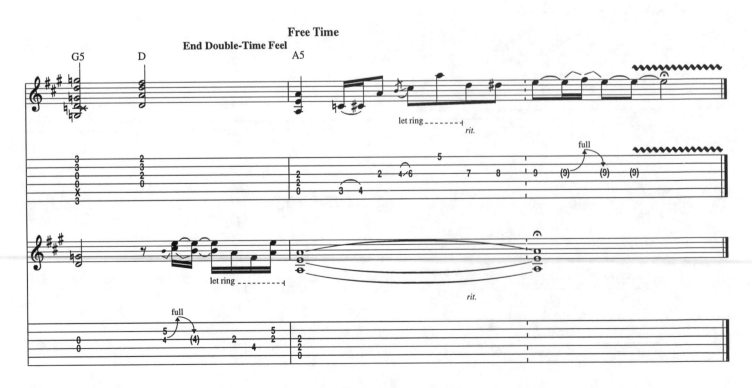

If You Want My Love

Words and Music by Rick Nielsen

it.   I won't throw _ your love _ a - way, _____   oo. ___   If you want _

%% Chorus

Gtr. 1: w/ Rhy. Fig. 1, 1st 7 meas., simile

___ my love _____ you got it.   When you need ___ my love ___ you got

it.   I won't hide it.   I won't throw _ your love _ a - way, _____   oo. ___

%% %% Verse

1. Yes, I thought you were a mys-ter-y girl, _   a spe-cial girl in this cra - zy old _ world.
2. You have the se-crets of love _ in this world. _   I'm hyp-no-tized by your ev - 'ry word. _

let ring throughout
2nd time simile

*Chord symbols reflect implied tonality.

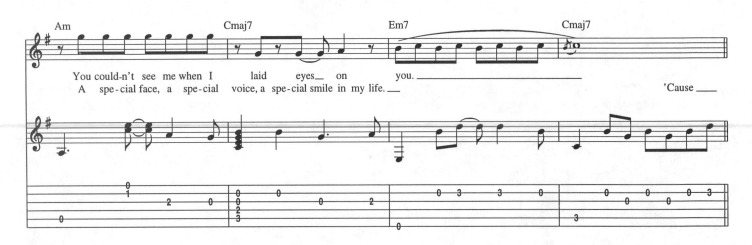

You could-n't see me when I   laid eyes _ on you. _____
A spe-cial face, a spe-cial voice, a spe-cial smile in my life. _   'Cause ___

Pre-Chorus

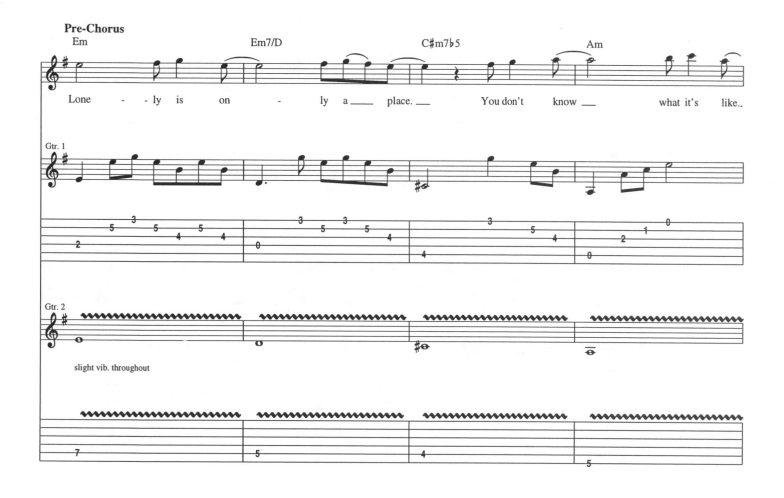

Lone - -ly is on - ly a ___ place. ___ You don't know ___ what it's like..

slight vib. throughout

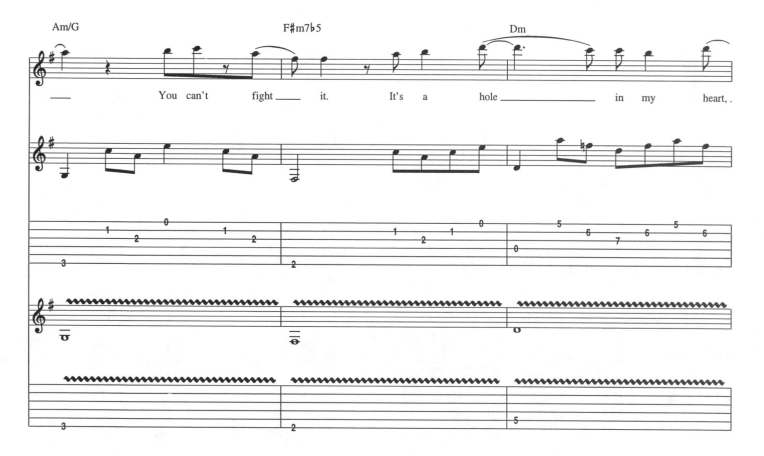

___ You can't fight ___ it. It's a hole ___ in my heart,.

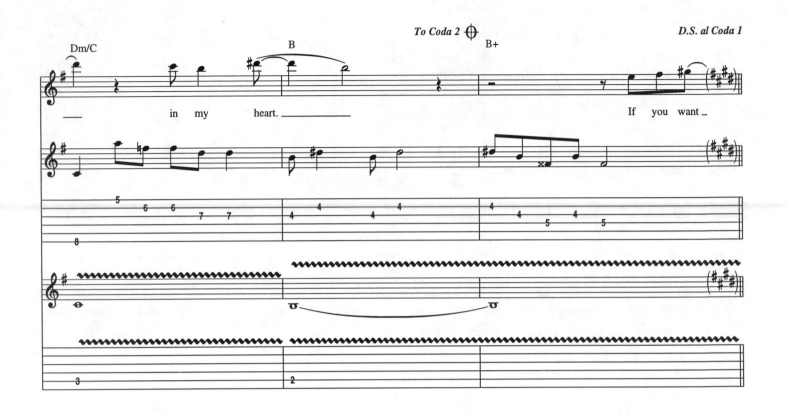

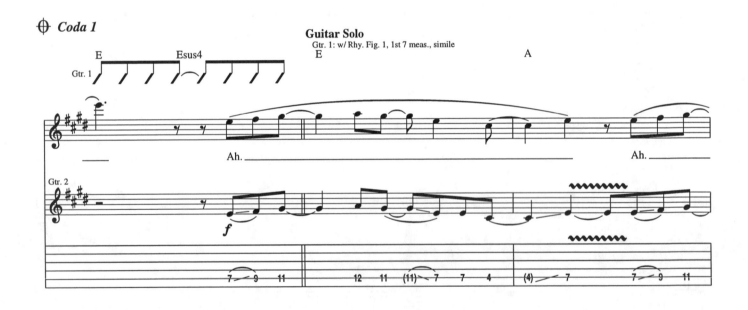

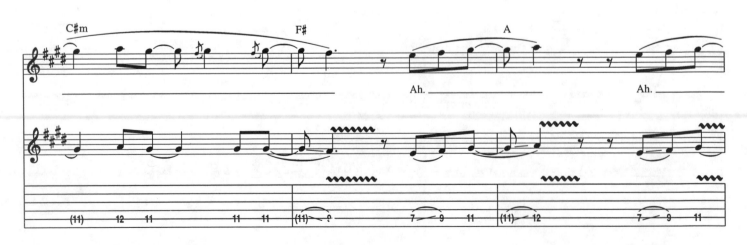

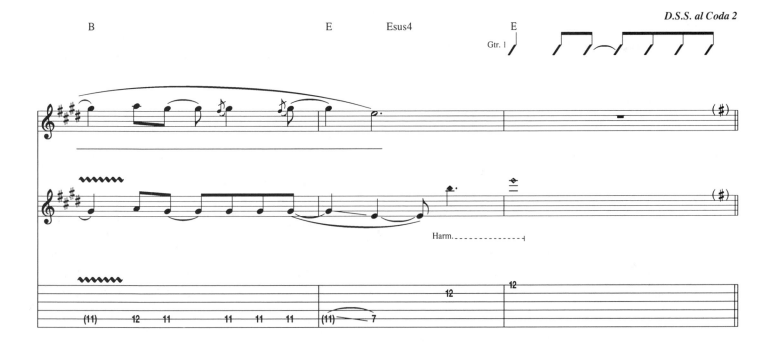

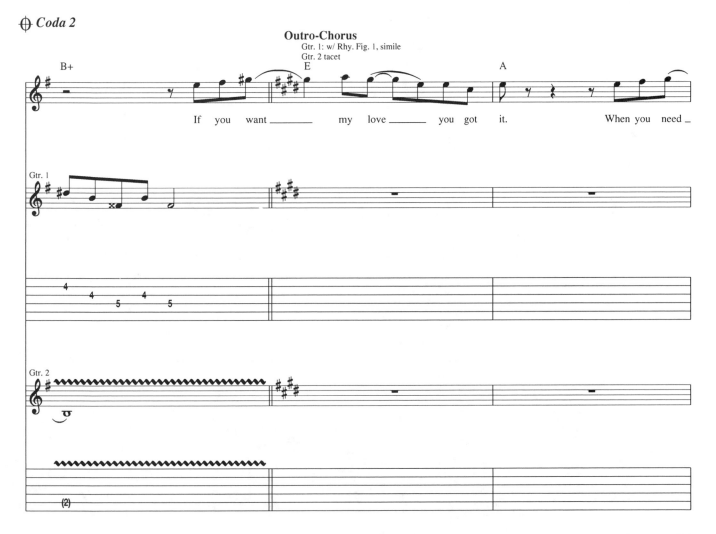

_my love _ you got it. I won't hide it. I won't throw_

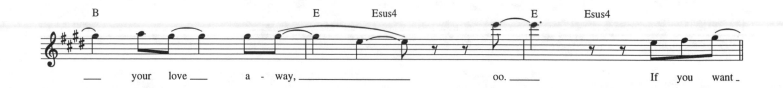

_your love _ a - way, _____ oo. ____ If you want_

Gtr. 1: w/ Rhy. Fig. 1, simile

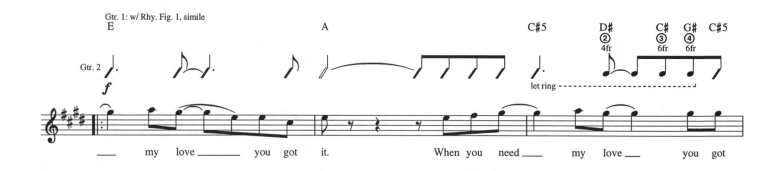

_my love ___ you got it. When you need ___ my love ___ you got

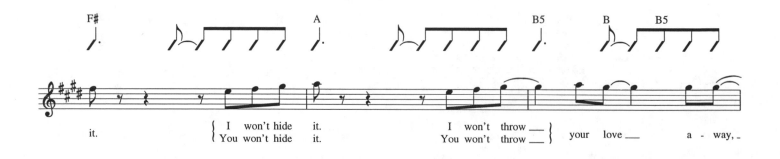

it. { I won't hide it. / You won't hide it. } { I won't throw ___ / You won't throw ___ } your love ___ a - way,_

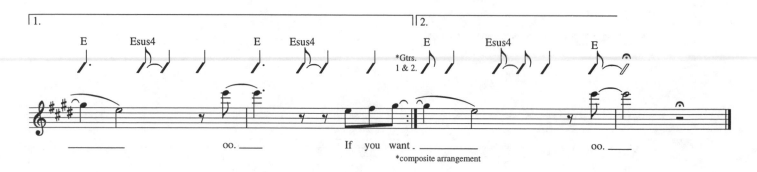

_____ oo. _____ If you want _ _____ oo. ____

*composite arrangement

She's Tight

Words and Music by Rick Nielsen

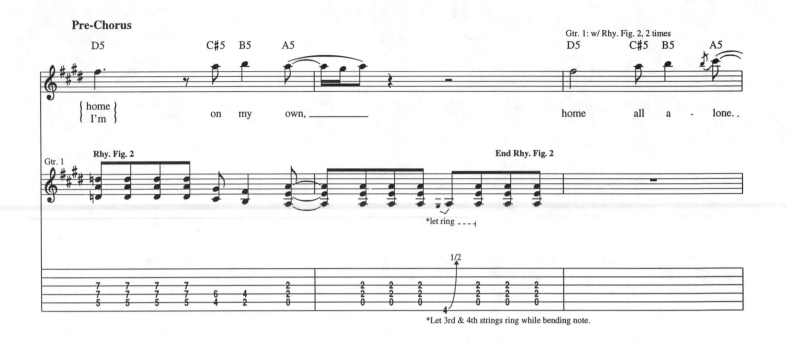

Pre-Chorus

home / I'm ... on my own, _____ home all a - lone...

let ring

*Let 3rd & 4th strings ring while bending note.

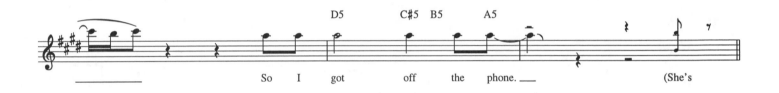

So I got off the phone. ___ (She's

Chorus

tight.) She's a - head of her time. ___ (She's tight.) She's ___ one of a kind. _ (She's

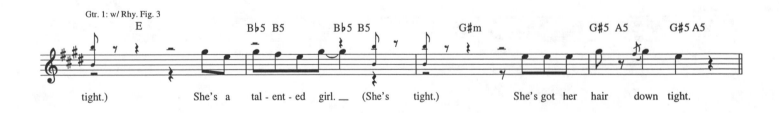

tight.) She's a tal - ent - ed girl. ___ (She's tight.) She's got her hair down tight.

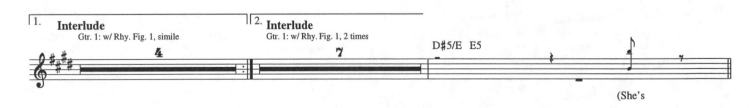

Interlude

(She's

Chorus

tight.)   She's   giv - ing me the go. (She's tight.)   She's giv - ing me the high sign. (She's

tight.)   We'll   turn off the lights.___ (She's tight.)   Pull   down   the shades. ___ (She's

Gtr. 1   Rhy. Fig. 4   End Rhy. Fig. 4

let ring ----------

Gtr. 1: w/ Rhy. Fig. 4, 2 times

nice, she's tight.)   Turn on the cam - 'ra. _ (She's nice, she's tight.) And get - ting read - y for ac - tion. (She's

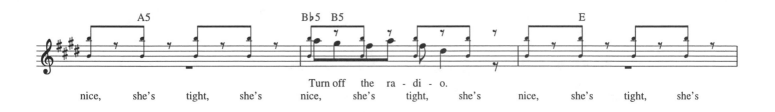

Turn off the ra - di - o.

nice, she's tight, she's nice, she's tight, she's nice, she's tight, she's

Interlude

Gtr. 1: w/ Rhy. Fig. 1

Turn   on   the   vid - e - o.

nice,   she's   tight.)   (She's

Outro Chorus

Gtr. 1: w/ Rhy. Fig. 3   *Repeat and Fade*

She's   giv - ing me the go. ___   She's   giv - ing me the high   sign. _

Turn out the lights.___   Pull   down   the shades. ___

nice, she's tight.)   (She's nice, she's tight.)   (She's

Southern Girls

Words and Music by Rick Nielsen and Tom Petersson

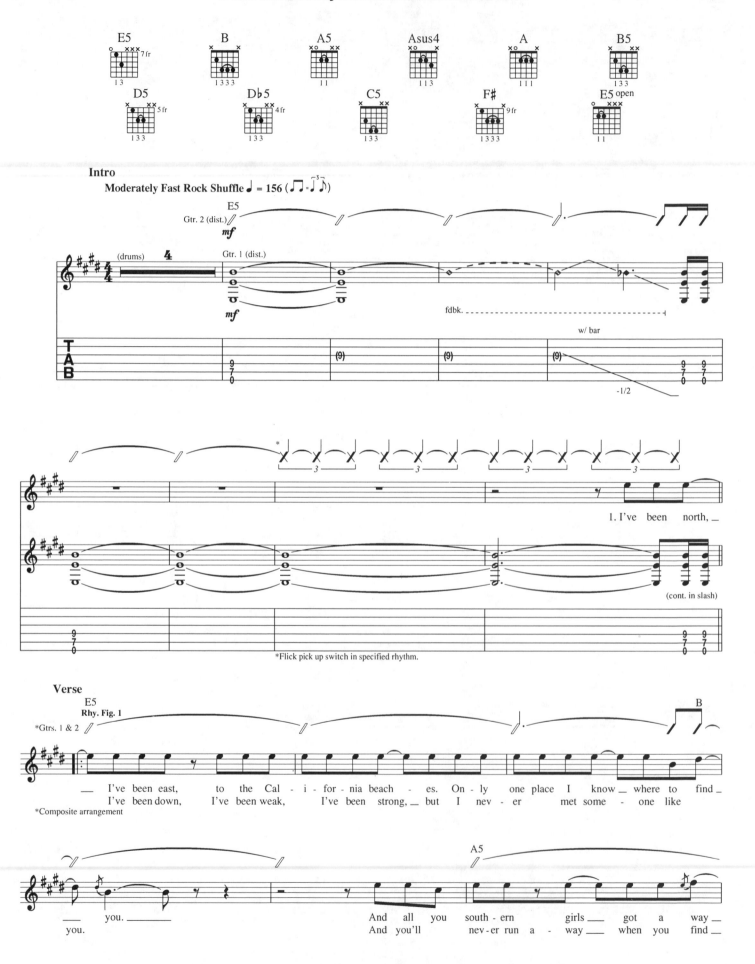

rock___ me___ and I'm cra - zy, and ev - 'ry - one says ___ it.
(Oo._____

South - ern girls, _____ you got noth - ing to lose. _____)

South - ern girls, _____ you got noth - ing to lose.
(Oo. _____)
2. I've been up

__)

Interlude
Straight Rock Feel

*bass plays B

Rhy. Fill 3
Gtrs. 1 & 2

Surrender

Words and Music by Rick Nielsen

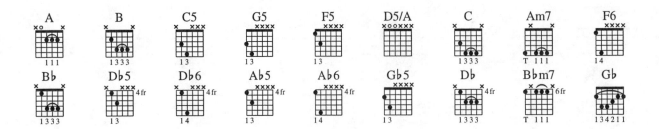

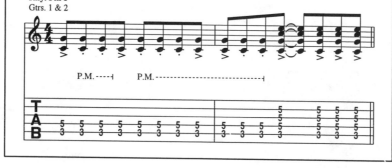

Chorus

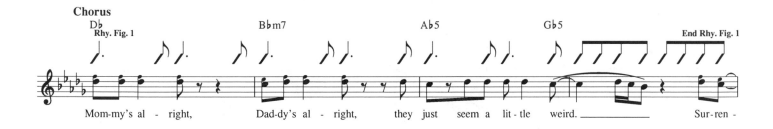

Mom-my's al - right, Dad-dy's al - right, they just seem a lit - tle weird. _____ Sur - ren -

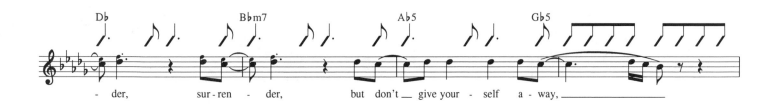

- der, sur - ren - der, but don't __ give your - self a - way, _____

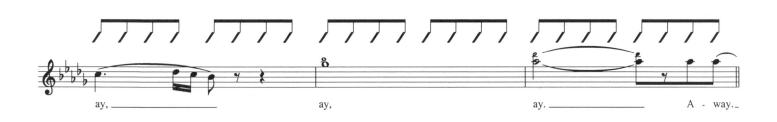

ay, _____ ay, ay. _____ A - way. ____

Bridge

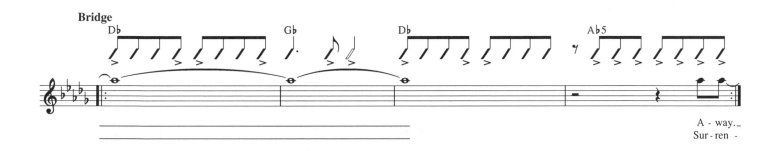

A - way. ____
Sur - ren -
A - way. __
Sur - ren -

Outro-Chorus

Gtrs. 1 & 2: w/ Rhy. Fig. 1

Play 7 Times and Fade

- der, sur - ren - der, but don't __ give your - self a - way. _____ Sur - ren -
(Mom-my's al - right, Dad-dy's al - right.)

83

Voices

Words and Music by Rick Nielsen

Guitar Solo

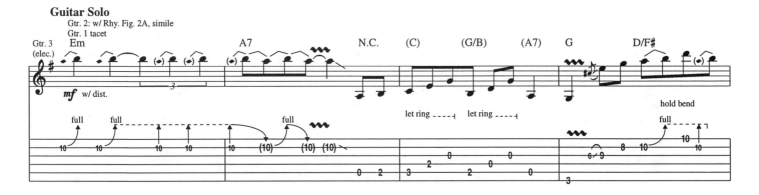

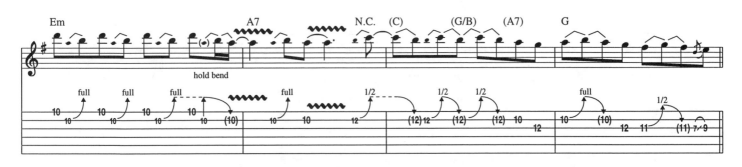

Bridge

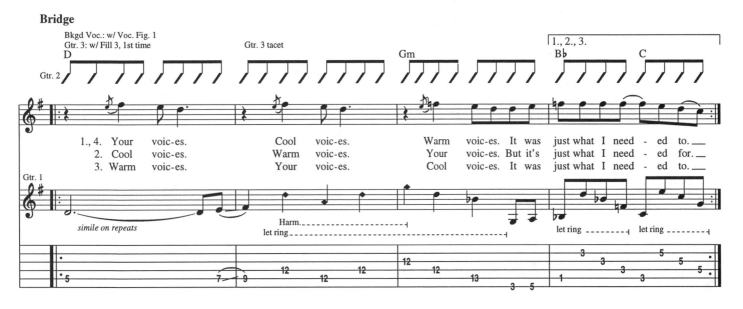

1., 4. Your voic-es. Cool voic-es. Warm voic-es. It was just what I need-ed to. ___
2. Cool voic-es. Warm voic-es. Your voic-es. But it's just what I need-ed for. ___
3. Warm voic-es. Your voic-es. Cool voic-es. It was just what I need-ed to. ___

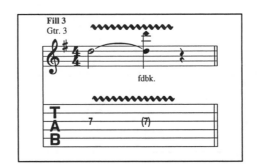

Fill 3
Gtr. 3

fdbk.

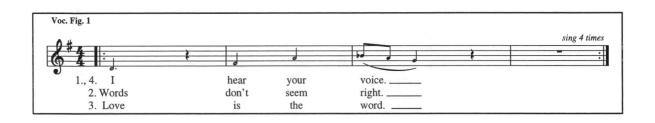

Voc. Fig. 1

sing 4 times

1., 4. I hear your voice. ___
2. Words don't seem right. ___
3. Love is the word. ___

Outro-Chorus

Gtrs. 1 & 2: w/ Rhy. Figs. 2 & 2A, simile
Gtr. 3: w/ Fill 4, 2nd time

2nd time, Fade Out

You did-n't know what you were looking for ____ till you heard the voic-es in your ear. ____

Gtr. 3

mf w/ clean tone

Begin Fade

You did-n't know what you were looking for ____ till you heard the voic-es in your ear. ____

Fill 4
Gtr. 3

Woke Up with a Monster

Words and Music by Rick Nielson, Robin Zander and Tom Petersson

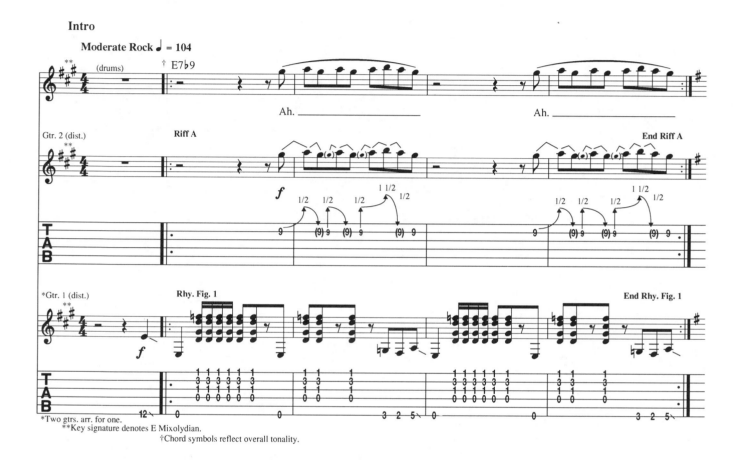

*Two gtrs. arr. for one.
**Key signature denotes E Mixolydian.
†Chord symbols reflect overall tonality.

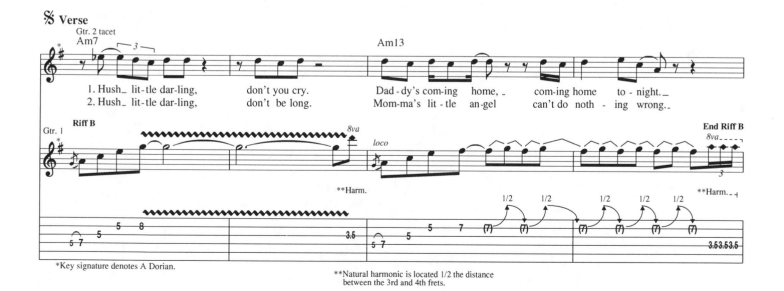

*Key signature denotes A Dorian.

**Natural harmonic is located 1/2 the distance
between the 3rd and 4th frets.

Bridge

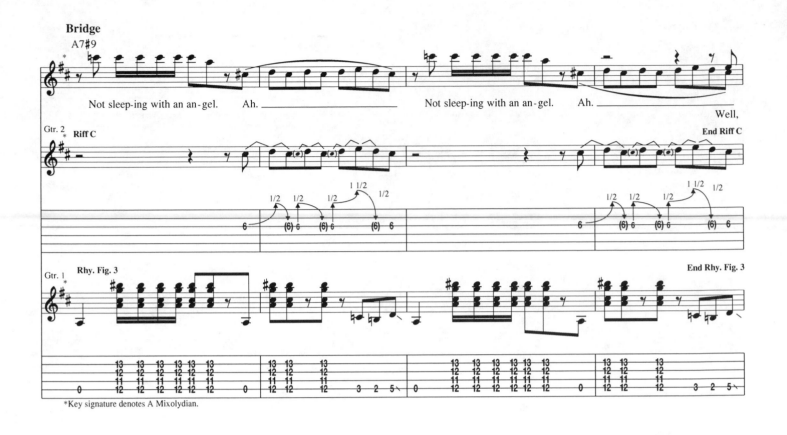

Not sleep-ing with an an-gel.   Ah. _____   Not sleep-ing with an an-gel.   Ah. _____

Well,

*Key signature denotes A Mixolydian.

Gtr. 1: w/ Rhy. Fig. 3
Gtr. 2: w/ Riff C

Mom-my and Dad-dy don't   see   eye__ to eye.   Mom-my and Dad-dy don't   hear when we cry.

Guitar Solo

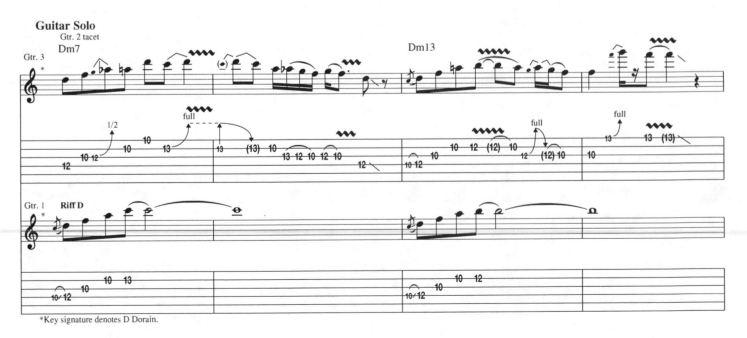

*Key signature denotes D Dorain.

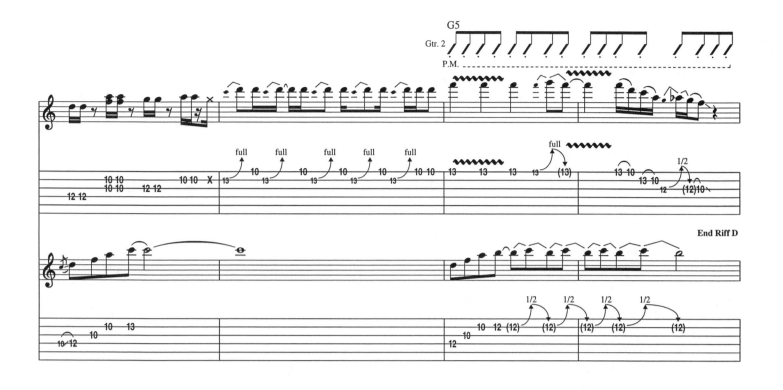

End Riff D

Gtr. 1: w/ Riff D
Gtr. 2 tacet

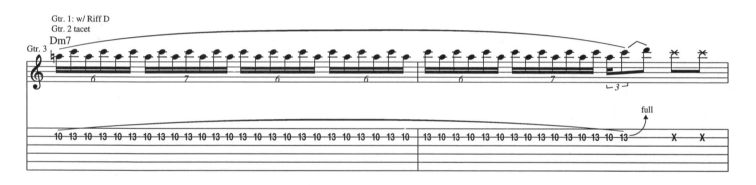

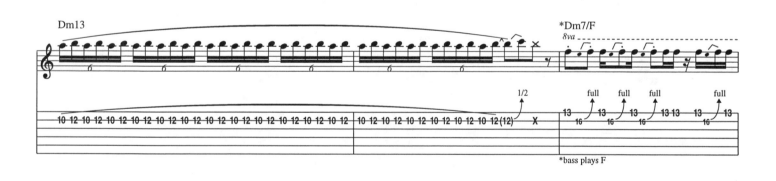

*bass plays F

D.S.S. al Coda 2

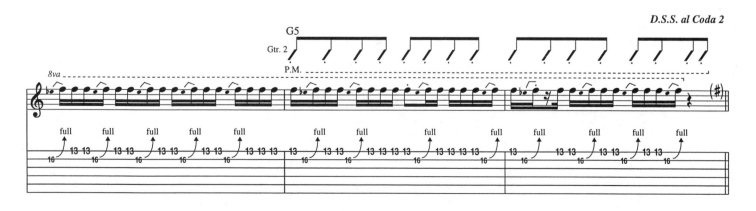

Guitar Notation Legend

Guitar Music can be notated three different ways: on a *musical staff*, in *tablature*, and in *rhythm slashes*.

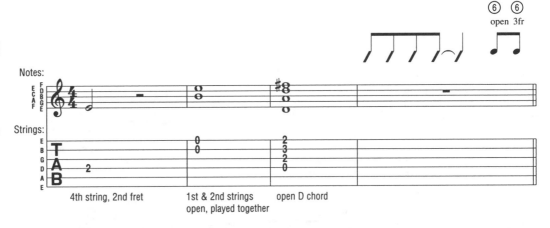

RHYTHM SLASHES are written above the staff. Strum chords in the rhythm indicated. Use the chord diagrams found at the top of the first page of the transcription for the appropriate chord voicings. Round noteheads indicate single notes.

THE MUSICAL STAFF shows pitches and rhythms and is divided by bar lines into measures. Pitches are named after the first seven letters of the alphabet.

TABLATURE graphically represents the guitar fingerboard. Each horizontal line represents a a string, and each number represents a fret.

Definitions for Special Guitar Notation

HALF-STEP BEND: Strike the note and bend up 1/2 step.

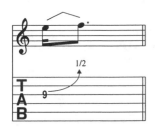

WHOLE-STEP BEND: Strike the note and bend up one step.

GRACE NOTE BEND: Strike the note and bend up as indicated. The first note does not take up any time.

SLIGHT (MICROTONE) BEND: Strike the note and bend up 1/4 step.

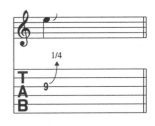

BEND AND RELEASE: Strike the note and bend up as indicated, then release back to the original note. Only the first note is struck.

PRE-BEND: Bend the note as indicated, then strike it.

PRE-BEND AND RELEASE: Bend the note as indicated. Strike it and release the bend back to the original note.

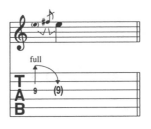

UNISON BEND: Strike the two notes simultaneously and bend the lower note up to the pitch of the higher.

VIBRATO: The string is vibrated by rapidly bending and releasing the note with the fretting hand.

WIDE VIBRATO: The pitch is varied to a greater degree by vibrating with the fretting hand.

HAMMER-ON: Strike the first (lower) note with one finger, then sound the higher note (on the same string) with another finger by fretting it without picking.

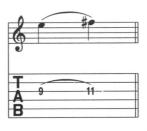

PULL-OFF: Place both fingers on the notes to be sounded. Strike the first note and without picking, pull the finger off to sound the second (lower) note.

LEGATO SLIDE: Strike the first note and then slide the same fret-hand finger up or down to the second note. The second note is not struck.

SHIFT SLIDE: Same as legato slide, except the second note is struck.

TRILL: Very rapidly alternate between the notes indicated by continuously hammering on and pulling off.

TAPPING: Hammer ("tap") the fret indicated with the pick-hand index or middle finger and pull off to the note fretted by the fret hand.

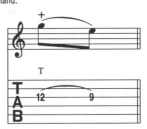

NATURAL HARMONIC: Strike the note while the fret-hand lightly touches the string directly over the fret indicated.

Harm.

PINCH HARMONIC: The note is fretted normally and a harmonic is produced by adding the edge of the thumb or the tip of the index finger of the pick hand to the normal pick attack.

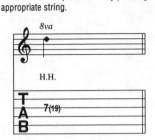

P.H.

HARP HARMONIC: The note is fretted normally and a harmonic is produced by gently resting the pick hand's index finger directly above the indicated fret (in parentheses) while the pick hand's thumb or pick assists by plucking the appropriate string.

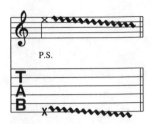

H.H.

PICK SCRAPE: The edge of the pick is rubbed down (or up) the string, producing a scratchy sound.

P.S.

MUFFLED STRINGS: A percussive sound is produced by laying the fret hand across the string(s) without depressing, and striking them with the pick hand.

PALM MUTING: The note is partially muted by the pick hand lightly touching the string(s) just before the bridge.

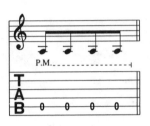

P.M.

RAKE: Drag the pick across the strings indicated with a single motion.

rake

TREMOLO PICKING: The note is picked as rapidly and continuously as possible.

ARPEGGIATE: Play the notes of the chord indicated by quickly rolling them from bottom to top.

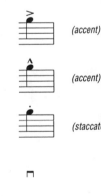

VIBRATO BAR DIVE AND RETURN: The pitch of the note or chord is dropped a specified number of steps (in rhythm) then returned to the original pitch.

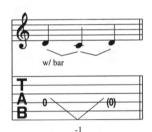

w/ bar

VIBRATO BAR SCOOP: Depress the bar just before striking the note, then quickly release the bar.

w/ bar

VIBRATO BAR DIP: Strike the note and then immediately drop a specified number of steps, then release back to the original pitch.

-1/2

w/ bar
-1/2

Additional Musical Definitions

(accent)	• Accentuate note (play it louder)	
(accent)	• Accentuate note with great intensity	
(staccato)	• Play the note short	
⊓	• Downstroke	
∨	• Upstroke	
D.S. al Coda	• Go back to the sign (𝄋), then play until the measure marked "**To Coda**," then skip to the section labelled "**Coda**."	
D.S. al Fine	• Go back to the beginning of the song and play until the measure marked "**Fine**" (end).	

Rhy. Fig. • Label used to recall a recurring accompaniment pattern (usually chordal).

Riff • Label used to recall composed, melodic lines (usually single notes) which recur.

Fill • Label used to identify a brief melodic figure which is to be inserted into the arrangement.

Rhy. Fill • A chordal version of a Fill.

tacet • Instrument is silent (drops out).

• Repeat measures between signs.

1. 2. • When a repeated section has different endings, play the first ending only the first time and the second ending only the second time.

NOTE: Tablature numbers in parentheses mean:
1. The note is being sustained over a system (note in standard notation is tied), or
2. The note is sustained, but a new articulation (such as a hammer-on, pull-off, slide or vibrato begins, or
3. The note is a barely audible "ghost" note (note in standard notation is also in parentheses).